Homecoming
poems of time and place

DAVID DONALDSON

THE CHOIR PRESS

Copyright © 2025 David Donaldson

All rights reserved. No part of this publication may be reproduced or transmitted in any form or by any means, electronic or mechanical including photocopying, recording or any information storage or retrieval system, without prior permission in writing from the publishers.

The right of David Donaldson to be identified as the author of this work has been asserted by him in accordance with the Copyright, Designs and Patents Act 1988

First published in the United Kingdom in 2025 by
The Choir Press

ISBN 978-1-78963-491-4

Contents

Origins 1

from A Glastonbury Sequence 2
Avalon 2
Paradise in Retreat 4
The Two Streams 5
In the Presili Hills 6
Enter the Palaeolithic 7
Tintagel 8
Arthur 10
The Yew Trees of Discoed 11
What Do You Seek? 14
Fossil-Hunting 15
Boiling Well 16
The Homecoming 18

Elements 19

Ice 20
Mountain Torrent 22
Sea on a Stormy Night 24
Storm Wind 26
Crop Circle 28
Crop Circle: Aerial View 30
Poem at Hallowe'en 31
Fire 32
Sky-Blue 34

Making 35

Flint	36
'Rain, Steam, Speed'	38
The River and the Mill	39
Bread	40
Transition	41
The Pace Quickens	42
Coldharbour Mill	43
King Coal and Welsh Miners	46
Requiem for Steam	47
Silicon	48

Messages and Warnings 49

Caesar's undelivered Message	50
Hadrian's Wall	51
Augustine's Chair	52
St Cuthbert and the Ravens	54
At Wenlock Priory	55
Message from the Bottle-Nose Whale	56
Who's to Blame?	58
Cathedral Healing Hour	59

War 61

Rome Triumphant	62
In Conclusion	64
Iron: Metal of Mars	65
Iron Gate	65
Ypres 1916	66
Descent into Hell	67
Aerial View	68
Partition	70

Pilgrimage · 71

- The Sea of Galilee · 72
- The Mount of Beatitudes · 73
- Mary's Dwelling? · 74
- Birthplace · 76
- Bethlehem · 78
- Creche Bethlehem · 79
- Baptism · 81
- Welcome Home · 82
- Jerusalem BC/AD · 84
- The Church of the Holy Sepulchre · 85
- *Hadrian's Podium* · 85
- *Constantine's Basilica* · 86
- *Christendom's Most Holy Shrine* · 87
- *November 2018* · 88
- Tabgha · 89

Times and Places · 91

- Walk in February · 92
- Man on Wire · 94
- Royal Wedding · 95
- Let's Riot · 97
- The Hallelujah Chorus · 99
- Golden Wedding · 101
- Fawley Church · 102
- 'Les Etangs' Revisited · 104

Notes and Acknowledgements · 108

Origins

from A Glastonbury Sequence

Avalon

To begin at the beginning.
The glassy Isles of Avalon,
Mirror of the heavens.
The seven stars of the Great Bear
Have alighted on its sacred hills
With Arth Fawr its guardian
And leader of the hunt.

Here, sky and earth unite.
Starry Draco's interposed
Between the Pole Star
And the Bear. Its serpent coils
Ring the Tor, guard the entrance
To the magic cauldron
Of the Underworld.

This is the Summerland,
Paradise of Perpetual Youth,
Isle of Apples set
In a silver sea as still
As dawn's awakening mystery,
Calm as the quiet plash
Of our paddling canoes.

Every hill, spring, stream
And grove speaks its part
Of a star-lit story,
Weaves into the narrative
Of the circling year
As the Bear circles the Pole
And our pilgrim wanderings

Return us to the beginning:
To these blessed Isles of Home,
Mothering sanctuary,
World's Centre where Earth
And Heaven are one, all's
Virgin abundance,
All endings, endlessly renewed.

Paradise in Retreat

The Earth lets slip her silver
Watery mantle. The roots
Of the starry hills appear
Land joined to land. Does

The rainbow's promise hold
As sea levels fall? This
Is Paradise in retreat,
The Isles of the Blessed

Stranded high and dry
In shallow lake and marsh.
Now wandering will cease,
Arth Fawr decline the hunt,

The Great Bear turn into the Plough.

The Two Streams

Abel dreams on beneath
The overarching crown
Of the Tree of Life,
The wisdom-stories
Of the stars, the phases
Of the moon attuned
To the immemorial Round.

Cain awakens to a thirst,
A music of the Earth.
He looks to dare
Its mysteries, open up
The guarded treasure store,
Quit the wandering life.

At his word great trees
Are felled, the dark earth
Opened to receive the seed,
Yield up its precious ores.
One river splits into two
Streams: one white, the other

Red with Abel's blood.

In the Presili Hills

Pembrokeshire

Widespread patches of marsh;
Sheep noses down among the gorse.
A scattering of giant stones

Appearing to lie just where
They've always lain and somehow
Familiar to us, having laboured

Over millenia to raise stones upright,
Gather them into avenues, circles
As if, in raising them, we aligned

Our being with the greater World,
Attuned it to the revolving harmonies
Of Sun, Moon, Stars, knowledge

Set to sustain our Earthly life within
The cosmic Round. And so, what lingers
In this still-strewn landscape, is a depth

Of silence as pristine-familiar,
                    as it is remote.

Enter the Palaeolithic

Trois Freres, 20 July 1914

Passages so narrow-low you have to
Squirm to move along arms tucked close,
Chins to the earth. Once able to stand,

You breathe out into pitch darkness,
Spellbound stillness. What light you strike
Cannot penetrate the cavern's height,

But spectral shapes forming out of the folds
And ridges on the walls appear: bison, bear
Picked out in charcoal, ochre; stalactites

Become antlers, trunks of mammoths,
Shaggy coats fashioned out of calcite;
Hybrid beasts with eyes of owls, bears' paws,

Human beards; ancient vision restored
To rational humanity on the brink
Of its first World War. Cryptic memorials

From ages of retreating ice, navigating
Spirit-worlds, trials in deepest darkness,
Inner journeys crossing all rock-bound

Thresholds of fear.

Tintagel

The twilight of the gods
Finds no foothold here: no
Tragic solemnity of loss,
Death darkening the skies,
Extinguishing the stars.

Here, inspiration's as ageless
As the elements: the sea
Seething about the rocky
Promontory, its cavernous
Boom in Merlin's cave

Sounding out the rocks'
Foundations or revealing
In its sudden surge and fling
Of spray, the gleaming
Iron-rich treasures
Of the volcanic rocks.

It's a place of origins.
There's no faltering in these
Widths of sea and sky
The light in constant interplay
With sweeping shadows,

Ever-shifting cloud formations,
Driving wind and rain
Or squally showers
Which unveil the rainbow
Overarching the distances

Or shimmering briefly
In a waterfall's mist-blown spray.
It's Arthur's fabled birthplace:
Within a mile, nine springs well up,
Earth brimful to overflowing,

The shape-shifting elements
Writ large around the year.

Arthur

at Glastonbury

Spans our history; giant slayer of old,
King of mythic conquests, heroic
Ordeals; Bran's son (or brother?)
Versed in bardic lore, fearless leader
Of perilous quests into the Otherworld.
The land's still strewn with his stones,

His quoits, his hill seats and earthwork
Round tables; and the caves and hollow hills
Where he and his knights still sleep until
The Great Awakening. Only the devil's
More inscribed in our landscape's
Memory. Our monarchs have seen fit

To claim his lineage and only Glastonbury
His grave. That master-stroke of royal
Expediency, to dig 'him' up and move him
To their chosen spot to rest! Yet still no
Arthur's ever lived to make it to the throne-
Nor ever will. Until *The Great Awakening.*

The Yew Trees of St Michael's Discoed, Powys

A Celebration

Mute companions. Both betray
Their ages. A trunk hollowed
And split like a foundered ship
In danger of breaking up;

Or sections of twisted naked boughs
That have long done with living.
Yet on they sail, serenely rooted
To the spot, leaving the gnarled

And crumbling wake of their
Longevity for us to wonder at,
The vigour of their regenerating lives
Lifting them like a never-failing tide

To sally forth in clusters of bright
New shoots, thrusting forces
As redoubtable and far-reaching
As the longbows their branches

Yielded in the recent past.

*

Elders. Aboriginal to the land.
Their roots touch into a dream-time
That peopled Albion with giants.

The megalithic avenues of Avebury,
The stirrings of Stonehenge
Shared their sapling infancies.

Their green childhoods witnessed
The first flashes of daylight
On worked metals: shooting sparks

Not of the night sky but from the bright
Blows of hammer on anvil. As youth
Advanced to age, so too the *Matter*

Of Britain. Excalibur, wrested from
The dull stone to rid the land of wrong,
Temper it in the fire of chivalry

And the self-transforming Quest
 Of the Holy Blood.

*

Who knows when we were drawn
To ring about this hillside patch,
Come here as to an unpolluted well

To drink? Still they speak to our
Troubled matters, first reaching
To the sky with their mysteries

Of the rising sap inwoven
With Earth, Moon and Stars-
And our own island beginnings;

From roots and trunk through
Millennia of discarded wood
To these still living, pliant, green,

Regenerating shoots!

What Do You Seek?

In response to Ralph Hoyte's question:
'What do you seek in this place, Visitor?'

I seek for things to use:
Cave-wombs, dragons' paws,
The sea's workings; prospects
Which give out onto all the directions;

The curved lens of the horizon;
Glitter of light, wave-lap; the airy
Fashioning warmth of the sun.
I seek what is to hand:

Ore of legends, place-specific
Like metals; like them to be mined,
Won, worked through to a fitting form,
Burnished to a pure brightness.

I seek for things still in the making-
My own heart; this place of legend.
I seek a cool sheath of ocean spray
And a hard-bellied ray of light

For a sword. Call it Excalibur.
I seek its healing, double-edged,
For my own making or unmaking.
I seek for something that will serve.

Tintagel

Fossil-Hunting

Lyme Regis

The cliffs are a charnel house.
The frost is quarrying them.
Tons of shale, dislodged,
Slithered onto the beach, lie
Spread in brooding spoil heaps
Over the golden sand.

It's a free-for-all, scrambling
To rummage through the shales'
Splintered leaves as if books
Tumbled from a Jurassic
Library had slipped both shelves
And bindings and scattered

Far and wide. Such treasures
Landed at our feet! Curled
Ammonites, pointed bellamites,
Grey lumps of fossil wood …
How to reconcile such
Remote antiquity with Now?

Our presence scrabbling
To prise them out, the wide
Sea at our backs, running up
Its smooth-mown lawn of sand
Lapping in playful calm;
As regular in ebb and flow

As the phases of the moon,
Or the constant steady beating
Of pulse and heart *Ah-*
(Whisper the humble fossils),
But it has not always been so.

Boiling Well

The Long Mynd, Shropshire

Wave upon wave. Crest upon crest.
The early Earth in movement come
To rest? Bony-backed ridges, jagged
Outcrops fused with sediments above
Their tumbled scree. One summit's
Smooth and rounded as an upturned bowl;
Another flattened like the blasted surface
Of an extinct volcano.

                      As far as the eye
Can see, all's fresh-clothed in green;
Stunted hawthorns clinging root-clasped
To steep valley sides are joining in the season
With their white may, and the white lambs
Browsing on the spring leaves as high
As they can. Skylarks, hard to pinpoint
In the blue, are taking up the song,
While, far beneath, on the valley floor,
A silver ribbon of stream is unwinding
On its way to the town that's like
A child's plaything nestling there below.

Such settled views! So at variance with
The accounts we reconstruct of past
Upheavals. What kind of kinship do we share
With land masses shifting in time-scales
We can't conceive; or with forgotten seas
And lands in ages-long repeated interchange?
Or those lost Worlds whose extinct creatures
Once roamed hereabouts and which we seek
To re-imagine from their fossilised remains?
And the ice sheets that ground these valleys
So steep and deep only to retreat uncovering
The tumultuous hills we see today; finally
At rest? Except for the mild refinements
Of temperate weathering with sun
And lark-song rising overhead, and valleys
Fed with streams ...

          Only ... once upon a time,
In wake of the retreating ice, this land
Re-emerged, clothed like a new World
In the making: *our World?* Wave-alive
In every motion of its boundless,
                      swaying trees.

The Homecoming

*Les Dents du Midi,
   Switzerland*

Rock calling to rock
From some undreamt-of
Depth of consciousness,
Blank-faced, immense.

The sheer drops unsettled
My sense of balance. Being
Upright felt presumptuous.
Eyes were safer lowered,

Each step placed with care.
Squeezing through a narrow cleft,
I found myself face to face
With overwhelming wastes,

Breathless heights, a World
Apart from the pastures
Left behind, gentians,
Harebells, ox-eye daisies,

Wooded slopes, the lake's
Sparkling life below. It seemed
That life itself had fallen
Out of time and mind.

What kinship here with skin
And bones and eyes?

Elements

Ice

Grips. Holds fast, while itself
Affording no grip, smooth
As glass; Water's transformed
Liquidity, become brittle,
Crystal-hard, miles thick,
Wafer-thin; always breaking

The rules: the lighter for
Its density and so bouyed up,
To float, to spread more like
A protective skin, than a winter
Depth-charge freezing to death
Whatever's living underneath.

Ice, for all its frost-bite cannot
Quite relinquish Water's service
To life, neither at the Poles nor
When taking Earth prisoner
In permafrost. Its grip remains
As in reflected service

To the once-living forms
Of creatures long since sucked
To suffocate in swamps before
Its arrival: as in Siberia beside
The Yuribey River, where
Lyuba (a baby mammoth),

Having taken a wrong step
Some forty thousand years ago,
Was discovered frozen-intact,
Near perfect; lying in her ice-
Tomb as if just having
                    drifted off

to sleep.

Mountain Torrent

white water in its joy of thunder
        whirling
  out of rocky crevices,
               pirouetting over
tilted glassy surfaces,
          tumbling
            down
                rapids
                      any-old-how,

a chattering jostling lather of bubbles;

some spin off,
    reeling into shallows,
  jolt up-and-down
          to vanish in a blink

while the roaring mass,
          lassoed into line,
                shoots off
to plunge over the next big dip;

carnival chaos,
        swelling as it cavorts along,
    and rocks unmoved,
    in the middle of it all;
  one face lathered, gleaming,
    another dull and dry;

others, breasting the chaos
                at a slope
                        receive
perpetual massage from the bubbling flow,
usher crowds
        helter-skelter
                over waterfalls
   or provide in midst of wildest tumult,
 overhangs
for trickles to wend their ways
                    and rows
                        of solitary drips
                                to take turns
                                    at making
inaudible
        plops
                and
                        plips.

Sea on a Stormy Night

Claws grappling
With the slippery surface
Of the sea wall, the salt-
Corroded iron of the railings

And slipping back,
Or pools of water suddenly
Gobbed up falling onto
The car park with a slap.

We dodge, laughing, dare
Venturing to the windy edge,
The foaming monster
Furious in full cry,

Pounding, plundering, its roar
The guttural of caverns
Vast enough to swallow
Our cathedrals at a gulp.

We peer down in the brief
Lull as the backwash
Uncovers rocks and steps,

Retreats to the main
As if inhaling one more
Gigantic breath for another

Rush, exploding against
Our defences. Boom
Answers our temerity,

Spray drenches us
Before we can back away;
Almost sweeps us off our feet,

Makes us gasp for breath,
Caught in the antics
Of our complacency.

Wake up! The sea plays
No games. The wild wind
Spares no thought for your security.

Lyme Regis

Storm Wind

We can't sleep through this performance:

The wind's hysterical, lost to wild extremes,
Its every screeching phrase punctuated
With a clanging dustbin lid. And rain

In fistfuls hissing, spitting against
The rattling windows like a cat
Clawing its way in.
                       All hell's
Let loose:
          bass notes booming down
The bedroom chimney, treble rising
Over the roof to a tearing shriek

And in the pauses, a groundswell of trees
Roaring in chorus like a heavy sea.

We lie in bed helpless, embroiled
In the madness: crescendos of grief,

Anguished howls as of souls in hell
All bluster blown to bits. There's no rest

From fearful imaginings: the wild gust
That will send the roof slates clattering,

Blow our windows in.

Charmouth, 19 December 1981

Crop Circle

Bryony Hill Hambledon 1990

A May evening humid and still.
Wind suddenly rustling the wheat,
The trees bending, a mist rolling
Towards us down Bryony Hill.

A whirlwind? But shimmering.
In seconds
we're encircled,
hair stood on end
pricked
head to toe with needles and pins,
can't
make ourselves heard for shrieking pan-pipes dinning the air

pressed down, sucked up,
spun from the path into the wheat,

held

                    as if
                   pinned
                as a circle's
               swept out from
              a centre of stalks
             forming a pyramid

             in part the whirlwind
             whirs on its way part
            whirls another circle nearby
            misty vortices inches apart
                     clear

to glisten like watery glass, lines quivering inside

                  across the field
there's a glowing tube endlessly funnelling into the sky

                minutes later, regaining the path,
                    ears throbbing, aching,

        we're drained

   amazed

                         in wonder

          in shock

Crop Circle: Aerial View

near Avebury, July 2008

A score of tiny figures casting shadows,
Arms outstretched as if willing wide
The doors of perception; nested within
The vessel of wheat, its swirled stalks
Bent, unbroken, laid precisely flat.

Scientists struggle to explain, hoaxers
Confess themselves surpassed, while
Explanations proliferate like the spread
Arrays year on year of these expressive
Beauties of form, galactic swirls and

Inter-weavings, complex geometric
Harmonies of such refined intelligence
They amaze, delight and baffle.
We're free to walk away, of course,
Just let be, or else –- return to figures

Such as these, casting their shadows below,
Arms stretched wide as if accepting
Here some wordless invitation to enter
Into communion with what cannot
Be denied, and their own unknowing.

Poem at Hallowe'en

The Sun has set aside its Summer glare,
Has gathered up the morning mist
   Like the folds of a white gown.

Now evening's falling, day already spent,
Leaves hang motionless, the least ruffle
   Of breeze could blow them down.

Stillness embraces all that breathes, settling,
Bringing thoughts to rest. The light's dying
     Fall sets our faces glowing,

In fond farewell it seems to say; the pain
Of leave-taking infused with promises
     Of Spring's renewed return.

Tonight is Hallowe'en, threshold of Winter.
Pray we never forget in stormy weather
   This lingering embrace that speaks

To the heart. May it remain there,
   Glowing, the Life of Light
   Throughout the Winter's dark.

Orcop, 2020

Fire

Memento Mori

You wouldn't know there was one
Burning out of sight at the bottom
Of the garden slope. The flames

Are flaring so hungrily, there's
Little smoke. It's storm damage
They're feeding on, fallen oak

And birch, the breeze stretching them
Forward into long tongues. It's
A funeral pyre, too: for a body

Of work from twenty years ago
Overdue for cremation. Scores
Of a collection overprinted

And long since reached its point
Of no return. You grasp the spines,
One at a time, open each book

Face down and drop it, spread-
Eagled into the blaze on top
Of the mounting heap of ash,

Until they're all consumed (except
For a few for old times' sake).
A trial run in contemplating

Fire's dealing with work that
Will no longer sell, and not
That merely- but your own

Material binding when its time
Has come for casting off
And that's reduced to ash

As well.

Sky-Blue

As day dawns, light
Calls up the songs of birds
And twilight-grey gives way
To the Sun's rising disc,

Its every blinding beam
Refracted in the clear
Crystal atmosphere to form
The perfect lattice of the sky.

Shoreless blue mediating
Day and night, Sun's light
Become life's sheltering
Airy canopy. Sky-blue

Evades all questioning;
The more we gaze,
The further it recedes
Even as it sounds on,

Raying from within,
Calling up, as dawn
The songs of birds, love
In every waking heart.

Orcop September 2019

Making

Flint

Bent to it, chipping away
Flake after flake with such
Determined focus, shaping
The rough core of the working self
As much as the rock, striking
With improving skill, finesse.

Painstaking labour of artisans
Winning through to the clear,
Sharp cutting edge, the piercing
Point of the arrowhead. Spoil
Heaps of discarded trials
Show the will that Flint ignites,

Grounding us in our tasks: tools
For hunting, cutting, scraping,
Striking sparks. It sent us
Delving into the Underworld
Inching forward in the dark
To search it out. It opened up

Distances for trade, strangers
Seeking exchange for it.
Issue of the Earth's crust
Seeping into limestone, chalk
From the primordial swell
Of seabed ooze, setting

To harden into cores of all-
Informing Silica: Flint's built
Into our foundations, still defines
Our earliest prehistoric Age;
There it lies in our fields, cast up
By the plough, rough nodules

Like forgotten spoils; or like this
Handaxe, (prized possession,
Spotted close to a rabbit warren),
Roughed out, unfinished- or
(More likely) discarded, failing
To make the grade from such

Exacting, raw beginnings.

'Rain, Steam, Speed'

*'Visit soon lest the train should dash
out of the picture' (Critic's response to
Turner's painting when first exhibited
 in 1844)*

Fury of fire, smoke, steam. Iron
Moulded in the furnace of our brains,
Poured onto rails and hurtling
Towards us out of the elements.

At once we're onlookers
And passengers, having to make
Way or be drawn after in carriage
After open carriage breathless, waving.

To a shriek of steam, our past
Rears and veers away in panic. Fire,
Iron, steam: our new-made horse.
The future's to run on rails.

The River and the Mill

1

The Blackdown Hills to Uffculme, Devon

Rises in a marshy field in the hills,
A puddling spring of trickles
Feeling out a downward course.

Coalesces over a mile or two
Into a noisy brook carving its way
Through clay and soon to be joined

By others, so progress swells from
Brook to stream, a silver thread
Spun out of the hills connecting

Villages strung along its course,
Gathering power as it broadens,
Straightens, acquires River status

And the motive force, channeled
Into leats since Saxon times (and
Noted in Domesday), to power

    The Mill, to turn the wheel
    To grind the grain into flour.

2

Bread

Timeless the river's flow
Even as it twists and turns
Through days, years, centuries.

Our collective lives also:
Millers working the mill
So the ground grain spills

To fill the sacks to overflow;
From Earth-yield of sun and rain
To the threshed ear of grain

Ground to flour, and flour
Moistened with water again
In the kneaded dough

And brought to the fire,
So what's placed on the table
For us to eat is Water's life,

Earth's growing, Sun's rays,
Fire's heat, our working days
Gathered to the risen goodness

Of fresh-baked bread.

3

Transition: an Old World to a New

Sugar for the sweet of tooth; raw materials
For processing on scales beyond imagining:

New horizons in which to expand, new
Inventions to supply demand, ambitions

Limitless as the rewards to be acquired.

*

The Mill wheel stops, its heart-beat stilled,
A passing World as *the wealth of nations* brims

To the full on the rising tide of slavery.
Tremors shake and shift the ground beneath

The feet of English workers in their cottages.
They, no less, are driven out of house and home

As working ways collapse.

1797

Not so for Thomas Fox of Were and Co.
A new, a better World is in the air.

Rumours of war, invasion scares,
Money in short supply, are no

Impediments. He's well-grounded,
Can offer work to those displaced;

His credit's trusted locally, secured
On the woollen mills already birthed

And in production. When money's tight,
The Company issues promises to pay:

They're bought up, as now: Thomas
Has taken stock: *the buildings*

Are but middling but the stream is good,
He writes on issuing three thousand

Five guinea notes and others beside.
More than enough to secure the site

To power the Mill, to turn the wheel,
To set to work the new machinery

Transforming local fleeces into cloth.

4

The Pace Quickens

The river flows on through.
Its motive power increased
As a new Wheel's installed
To turn, turn as ever before

But the Mill's heart beats
To a difference pulse; urgent
Quickening year on year
As time appears to gather pace

And buildings rise five
Storeys high. To a shriek
Of steam the railway
Arrives in Tiverton.

And a lifetime's passed.

The New World's fledged
And spread its wings.
Horizons strive to reach
World-wide. The Mill
Embraces coal, fire, steam.

    5

Coldharbour Mill

1865-1981

Primordial Earth revives
To elemental life. Sunlight's
Deep-stored energy's released
To blaze and smoke. Water
Boils and writhes in steam;
Fiery lungs breathe motion
Into an engine's steel limbs
Greased against them seizing up.

Coal by the ton feeds the boiler.
Power increases twelve-fold
Over the years. The driving belt
Rumbles to the line-shaft
On all five levels at once
For *more, more, more* as below
The fires glow and smoke
Billows out on high.

Never enough, never enough
Rattle the trains on the shiny rails
Spreading out nation-wide.
Once smashed and vilified,
Machines now whirr and chatter,
Clang and clatter carrying all
Before them as the pace
Of *Progress* hurtles forward

Some tumultuous Mill-race
Headlong drawn to the brink
Of chaos; fire, steam, boiler
Swept aside as *Electricity*
Claims its plugged-in prize
(Though the river's flow turning
The waterwheel still works
The nights; until..) tired workers

Rub their eyes and make for home
As dawn breaks on the final shift.
In their wake, the deafening
Silence of a passing age.
Only warmth of heart and will
Are left to save the Mill from
Crumbling neglect, convert it
To museum-pace; as time

And the means allow, rouse
Its slumbering powers: fire up
The boilers, set rumbling the giant
Driving belt for the public
To admire; show off the clattering
Precise machinery transforming
Tons of raw material into such
Well-worn warmth and beauty

As the finished cloth.

King Coal and Welsh Miners

A Tribute after hearing Welsh Male Voice
Choirs in St. Mary's Church, Conwy

Free men, locked into their valleys' native riches.
Lives lived daily in the neighbourhood of death.
Generations bonded together in life-long service
To King Coal. Each early morning, sun or cloud,
To be lowered into earth's perpetual dark, working
The *coal face*, spellbound shining of the ancient sun,

Its blaze transformed from warming rays to sooty
Smoke and fog. Each evening, to surface again,
Seek rest beneath their labours' towering hills
Of waste, while trains rumbled on through the night
Bearing black gold to the holds of coal-fired ships,
To white hot furnaces of industrial Fire. And they,

Unbowed, though bent and bound in service
To Capital's mounting world-wide extractive fury,
Had yet more to pit their strength against than
The gleaming seams of the coal they worked.
How to wrest a living equal to all their
Herculean tasks required? And here, now?

What rises up to us, distilled as from those
Profound abandoned depths, is, *song:* men
Giving voice to hymns of faith, of praise.
The perils dared, the depths once delved,
The disasters that befell, sustained,
Lived through, upheld on such harmonies;

The swell of such collective breaths of song.

Requiem for Steam

Just over a century to come off the rails.
Be put to the cutter's torch. The billowing smoke
Like a creature breathing. Its sudden hisses
Quietening to the murmur of steam at rest.

Or the piercing whistle and plumes of smoke
Signaling the gathering effort to depart.
The crescendo of chuff upon chuff upon chuff
And the rattling music of the rails as the speed

Picks up. And the dim-lit carriage compartments.
Sooner or later we find ourselves at Adlestrop,
Those lazy country stations and lingering
Branch lines that had to close, flowering

Banks, and branches within arms' reach,
The curve of the single track an enticement
To stay looking out for what was to appear
Around the bend: the journey as much

    The intention as its end.

Silicon

Silicis: Latin for Flint

Pure extract of the Earth's crust,
All impurity of oxygen expelled.
See how it shines, our forged jewel
In its silvery suit! Newly received
Into our scheme of things: neatly

Placed: metalloid. Element 14:
Most prized of semi-conductors,
Hard-won purity first doped
To set in place a wealth of circuitry
Invisible to the naked eye

The better to bear such Data –
Volumes hurtling from God
Knows where, speeding up Time
Through Time's suspense,
Breaking into the breathing

Rhythms of lives from regions
We're driven to assume Thinking
Will always attain the mastery of.
Silicon! Crust of the Earth;
Once-upon-a-time, our pride

Was the raw, perfected cutting edge,
The piercing point of the arrowhead.
And wafer-thin flint chips we then
Let fall into spoil heaps. What Brave
New World as cold, hard, sharp-

Edged, are we inviting in?

Messages and Warnings

Caesar's undelivered Message

I am Caesar's messenger. We start without delay.
A winter's night. The dark clouds raced,
The wind whipped spray into the skipper's face.
The crew bent to the oars and fought their way.

The river's mouth was gained. As black as hell
Wild wind and sea beat breath away,
Foam flew. *We cross before the break of day.*
Wave-struck, the boat pitched and fell

Was driven back. Caesar's messenger rose,
Flung back his cloak. *Take courage! It is I
Caesar himself you carry as cargo. Try
His Luck. Strive forwards into the wind's blows.*

Amazed, as if a sudden comet had rent
The clouds with light and blazed a blinding trail
Across the heavens in proof they could not fail,
They set to, bowed to the oars, heads bent

In glad obedience to this lord of men
Who dared them to be more than themselves; trust in
His Luck to stem the storm, to veer the wind.
They yoked their fate to his fate then,

Laboured for hours in the churning seas
And only turned back as dawn broke grey,
Baulked by the greater perils of the day:
The watchful eyes of waiting enemies.

Hadrian's Wall

From the Pyramids to this far frozen sea
Of volcanic outcrops facing north:
Windswept loneliness of curlew, skylark-
This the full span of the Eagle Empire.

Blocks of sandstone quarried below
Were hauled to these steep heights.
From coast to coast a close-linked chain
Of signal towers, milecastles, forts

Awoke the native tribes to their one
Choice of lord and master: Rome,
Whose works and words of law
Defined the civilised and barbarian.

The swords of its enemies shattered
On its tempered Spanish steel,
Its weaponary penetrated every detail
Necessary to out-manoeuvre, overwhelm.

This its continuing legacy: those ever
More precise and calculated ways
Of thinking, that self-belief, that will
To power. And this Wall, now levelled

Low enough to be a child's challenge?
A strung necklace gilding the curves
And contours of the countryside amid
The unchanging calls of curlew, skylark,

Silent witness not only to this utmost
Extension of imperial will but also-
To reaches where that will could not prevail.

Augustine's Chair

The British and Roman Churches face to face
          A.D 603

A fine summer's day. Bees buzzing
About a crannied wall. A soft breeze
Playing in the full-dressed trees.

And a chair, placed in the shade
For Augustine's use, despatched
From Rome to set the Word

Resounding throughout the land
Of the Glastonbury Thorn.

    *

Reverberations! What was
The British Church, (set foot
On shore five centuries before)

To make of this? How to know
Such a man were truly sent
Of the Lord? *A man of God*

(Thus the hermit they consulted),
Is meek, not haughty or unbending,
Yes, but how were they to be sure?

Arrange matters so he's there already
When you arrive. Does he rise
To greet you as brother to brother?

If so, rest assured he is sent of the Lord.
And if not? If he remains seated?
Then take care! He thinks himself

    Your superior.

      *

A meeting of men on a tree-covered hill.
The Church of Rome first to come there.

How to arrange the meeting? After careful
Deliberation, a chair is sent for.

      *

Now, mounting the winding lane uphill, enter
Seven British bishops with their learned men,
Brushing the flowering grasses as they come.

Once out of the sun, their long journey done,
They pause for breath, prepare for the manner
Of the Roman greeting, smiles upon their lips,

Eager themselves to greet this friend in Christ?
One Gospel, differing pathways; one Meeting,
Two forces sparking storm. Frozen smiles?

Chilly silences? Frowns like gathering clouds
Beginning to overcast the sky? One hermit's
Wise words echoing on; one lightning flash

And rolling Roman thunderclap of warning
Prophecy sounding forth their different ways.
Who was right? Both! The prophecy came true,

Rome as immovable in conviction as the other
In humble foresight of what that simple failure
To rise would portend. There, in the chair

Unmoving,
      Augustine sat.

St Cuthbert and the Ravens

Black wings over Lindisfarne:
Two nesting ravens flying back and forth
From the hospice roof stealing the thatch.
Cuthbert gestures in protest but they
Continue unabashed- such rich pickings.

He bids them begone *in the name of Christ* –
And peace resumes. They take flight,
Cuthbert repairs the ripped up patch,
Gets on with his digging. A few days later,
Back bowed to the spade, he hears the stir

Of feathers, looks up: it's one of the pair,
Its black wings trailing the earth, muted croaks
Sounding from its downcast beak. Given leave,
It flies away, returns with its mate who drops
A hunk of lard at Cuthbert's feet. He accepts

The offering, uses it to grease his boots-
And draws a moral so old-fashioned, we smile
And shrug in disbelief, our own black wings
Spread wide over the world and we
Continuing unabashed: such rich pickings!

At Wenlock Priory

Stone on stone, this ruined place returns to life,
Resumes its working: Opus Dei, the shared
Vision and investment of the rich and powerful alike.

Dead weight of stone fashioned into life, raised
Skyward tier on tier and vaulted to be a home
Fit for the Spirit: to grow wings, to soar, to intercede,

Maintain the commonwealth in harmony with God,
Be as the kingdom's lungs, its continuous breathing
In and out: inhalation of the sacred Word,

Exhalation day and night in prayer and chant.
And so its life, intensified, rippled out:
A place dedicated to study and transcription

Of the Holy Book, to the disciplines of peace:
To learning, education, the healing arts,
Cultivation of the soil, stewardship of the land.

Around it grew the town which now lives on
Beside its ruins: vision, vows, sanctity of living
Long brought low by accumulated wealth,

Disputes with the Crown, burdens of debt,
Internal wranglings, abuses of its Rule: that lure
Of creature comforts now become so much

The rhythm of our daily lives, our world's commercial
Rule and, like this ruin, our roofless dream:
To continuously consume beyond our means.

Message from the Bottle-Nose Whale

died in the Thames, London, during January 2006

Thank you for the attention.
The special barge, the lifting gear.
It was all well meant. And those
Thousands of you crowding
The rails to see: Jonah's whale
Turned prophet, headed for
The dead-end reaches
Of your city, great Nineveh!

Thank you for your concern,
Your touching pity, your fervent
Wishes for me to live my way
Back to the ocean's freedom
And a happy ending. How
Relieved you would have been!
How pleased that your best efforts
Had succeeded. But it wasn't to be.

Do you understand? No amount
Of skills, gear, heart-felt well-
Meaning will ever be enough
While that bleaching deadness
Of disconnection you call
Thinking overrules all else. Why act
As if the likes of us did not exist?
Or must make way? For what?

The debts you are running up?
I hold up a mirror. Look into it.
You and your battling corporate
Heads swollen out of all proportion!
Infestation for us: rampaging
Over land and ocean, worse
Than the dinosaurs you're so
Sentimentally enamoured of;

Worse with your clever outsized
Machinery that infinitely inflates
Your greed. Oh, human beings!
You have Heart. *Grow it! Think
With it!* It's all you have to rein in,
Calm and guide your all-
Consuming, fearful, warring,
Misguided, overactive Head!

Who's to Blame?

The Haitian earthquake, January 2010

The houses collapsed according to natural law.
What followed was immutable: death and putrefaction.
The stench of unclaimed corpses fouled the air.
Reason says: this does not accord with a God of Love.

Yet days later, a baby's cry is heard. She's freed
Unharmed, handed into her mother's aching arms.
Life's a cruel lottery (says Reason), thousands buried
And here and there some miracle of relief and joy.

And worldwide people open their hearts and purses
To help put right what should never be. What might
It mean were Earth to be no more disaster-prone,
No more upheavals of land or sea, its inner fire

Contained, the very image of a sainted One
In self-command, its forces tuned in harmony?
Who's to blame? Look at the elemental Earth
As into an unflinching mirror. Were we truly

To grow in Love, might it not do the same?

Cathedral Healing Hour

… all Creation groaning in the pangs of birth …
(Romans 8)

And then the dog barked. It must have felt
Ill at ease on the cold stone floor or been
Pricked to protest by its owner's quiet distress,

Voicing, perhaps, his unvoiced plea for help
But in its dog's unknowing way, so sure
To be out of place. It barked down the human

As he read of all Creation groaning
In the pangs of birth. Stewards rose to manage
The situation: subdued voices echoing

In the massive darkness of the unlit nave.
Continued canine protests. Its owner took it
For a calming walk: dog in yellow jacket

Bypassing the waiting dozen gathered
Beside a saintly shrine and marble tombs:
But to no avail: unwilling to sit, lie, be still

For its owner's sake. So they left. The ritual
Resumed: resettled communion of calm,
Of shared attention- the anointing, quiet

Music.. and the echo of a dog entering
On cue as if reflecting back the words
Its barking had brought so abruptly to a stop.

War

Rome Triumphant

The Destruction of Carthage

Rome triumphant. Beyond the smoke
And the ploughed-in curse of salt,
The skies were clear to the blue horizon.
    Yet Scipio wept

An end declared. And a new beginning.
Wealth beyond imagining would soon
Come flooding in on the rising tide.
    Yet Scipio wept

There would be slaves for the asking,
Land beyond all previous measure,
Mercenaries to defend such hard-won treasure.
    Yet Scipio wept

Civic centres would arise. Paved streets,
Piped water, welfare of bread and blood-
Excitement for the poor, the dispossessed.
    Yet Scipio wept

Power would acquire imperial focus,
Caesar's rule extend for life, triumphal
Arches swell the heart with pride.
    Yet Scipio wept

What of the Republic's sturdy heart
Of simple homesteads, self-defended?
There would be Dominion, the Pax Romana,
    Yet Scipio wept

Note: Scipio Aemilianus, the Roman general responsible for the destruction of Carthage in 146 BC

In Conclusion

Hitler's Coming on the Clouds

   Night. His approach
     Signaled by lights
   In the sky, aircraft drone
Gathering to overpower

   As it descends. Railways
Laid to serve the ritual space
   Beating to a martial pulse
     Of welcoming bands,

   Multitudes pouring onto
   The platforms, streaming
   Towards the floodlit heart
Of the Fatherland, united

In the mystery of blood
   By the One arriving
     Out of the clouds.

The work begun by Christ,
   I will bring
To a conclusion, he says.

Words to ripen lethal fruit.
An audience magnetised.
   Its bearings lost.

Iron: Metal of Mars

Two poems inspired by an exhibition of ironwork in Hereford Cathedral, Autumn, 2017

Iron Gate

'The War to end all Wars'

This gate gives you pause.
Iron drops of blood hang
In suspense the length

Of its bars, earth-heavy
As if about to drip and fall;
While the bars themselves

Are crowned with leaves,
Blood's red transformed
To a waving riot of green.

Hope wrought in iron?
But should you wish
To lift the latch and enter,

There's no saying that
Simple switch of colour
Won't go into reverse:

Green leaves to red
Flames. Iron once more
Slipped out of control.

Ypres 1916

Barbed Wire

How he wished above all for mastery,
Heaved out the black coal, summoned
The elements, lit the furnaces and set

To work so that everything he touched
Turned to Iron. The very rocks wept
Tears of Iron. With them he spanned rivers,

Crossed oceans, laid continents to rail...
And how the Rule of Iron took possession,
His fingers forever pointing in command,

His fist always grasping to take hold until
Fist and fingers turned into barbed wire,
And a World died as the sky rained Iron.

How he'd wished above all for mastery,
Not a catafalque of scarlet poppies
Nor the white rows of the countless crosses.

Descent into Hell

Damascus, Syria

But what of human beings?
I ask again. What awakened life
For those not crushed to death,
Waking to find their homes
Bombed to rubble, their parents,
Their children, already dead?

Or those cowering in basements
Sheltering from missile showers,
Shrapnel rains, barrel-bomb
Thunderclaps? Accounted
Vermin to be flushed out
With chlorine gas into the lethal

Blaze of day? Or those a few
Minutes' drive away out shopping
To the distant impact of high
Explosives? Death being dealt
Elsewhere- over there; not
To them, not yet. What is Earth

To these if not *Hell* gaping
To conduct the lost and dead?
Small wonder we look on
Dumbstruck, helpless at the gates
Of Damascus, the steely zeal
Of lifeless thoughts in dead machines

To mock us. Oh, to emerge from
The grave of our skulls! Touch
Once more Life's seamless robe,
Gather beneath the healing shade
Of the Tree of Life whose leaves
(It's said) are *for the healing of the nations.*

Aerial View

A postcard of Frankfurt in March 1945

The sky's rained fire to abort the spring.
For once, facades cannot conceal
The truth: those left standing give out
Onto rubble. There's not a roof in sight.
Now night has given way to this forlorn
March day, what can be said but- watch,

Keep awake, as the hinterland in you
Parts to peer with fascination. Observe
What stirs: some inbred appetite, some
Deadly satisfaction at this deathly calm
Of ruin truly accomplished, and how
The self-perpetuating powers

Of our collective hell stand ever ready
To be fed our murderous fare, incite
Our iron to do its worst. Watch
As they worm their way into any
Interstice unsecured by goodwill:
So many choices of enemy!

Yet now, standing postcard in hand
In this bustling square, these same
Bombed-out facades whole buildings
Once more, a queue of tourists outside
The restored Town Hall, I'm witness
To the miracle of the Phoenix, fully

Fledged in new life, in prosperity.
If only that were that! So this postcard
Stands as counter-witness. As solemn
Warning to the cycles of destruction.
For the spoken words that laid
This city flat continue to slip off

Tongues and lips the world over:
Poles of fire and ice in us combining
To freeze and burn and forever
Scheme to overturn the uplifting
Balance of loving human warmth
And make our blood boil – or else run cold.

Partition

India 1948

Those placed to lead as figureheads
May serve with honour and integrity
Having no idea they're blinkered,
Their course determined in distant rooms
Where the maps are spread and boundaries

Redrawn by far-sighted ones in suits
Crystal-gazing a century ahead. Words
Of warning may be issued across
Polished tables and others spoken
To reassure and smooth the way,

For Advantage must be served to keep
The Enemy at bay. And so World Powers
Perpetuate World tragedies. A border fuse
Laid to a powder keg; civil disorder reigns
And millions fleeing for safety are either

Slaughtered or displaced.

Pilgrimage

Galilee to Jerusalem, November 2018

The Sea of Galilee

There! The Sea of Story, taken to heart
In hymns of church and chapel.
O calm of hills above. A lake- no sea
(But ancient Hebrew lacked the words)

The shoreline now in slow retreat
Uncovering remains that show rhythms
Of its human history not yet understood.
And sailing on it: cutting the engines

To allow the wide silence to drift over us
Our childhoods invested with story
After story: the sudden squalls,
The ordered calm, the empty nets

Now full to breaking and- the invitation
To walk on water. And our presence here
Turning stones to bread! A local livelihood
For many and our guide speaking

Of the sound of bombers heading over
The hills to blow up the suburbs of Damascus
Only a few miles away. And our boat
Rocking us as in a cradle, in silence.

The Mount of Beatitudes

Blessed with volcanic rock,
Iron fertility. Black heaps
On the slopes as we wind our way up.
The weather's turned out well
After the night's thunderstorm.

There's blue above,
The glittering haze of the Sea below.
Parrots in the palms
Making their presence known;
Varied blooms of bougainvillaea

And others I cannot name;
An old fig its roots poking up
Like bony shoulder blades,
Its branching shade blessing an altar
Where the air rings in harmony

As people sing. And we of the West
Blessed to mingle here with those
Of Asia, India, Africa. A steady flow
To and fro about this hilltop paradise
For as long as one's coach allows.

Let anyone who thirsts come to me and drink,
The verse declares inscribed on stone
Where a spring wells. Blessings…
All gratefully to be received.
But Christ's no Father Christmas.

Living water wells to grow humanity.
See the Beatitudes achieved.

Mary's Dwelling?

The Church of the Annunciation

    Completed in 1969

Basilica of antiquities uncovered
In its construction, each revered,
Traces preserved as predecessors;
Itself no antiquity: this, the fifth
Building on the site to hold high
The flame, successor to Franciscans,
Crusaders, Byzantine worshippers,

Until, finally, Greek letters scratched
On an unearthed stump of column
Spell out: XE MAPIA (*Hail Mary*)
And we've touched down into ancient
Nazareth, its silos, cisterns; a cave-
Dwelling (as here) railed off, three
Metres below the floor, the venerated

Rock-hewn cavern this most monumental
Of churches has been constructed for:
The unassuming site of young Mary's
Visitation; her family's dwelling itself?
(Or basement stable for their animals?)
Look up! A lantern cupola more than

Fifty metres above, spans the space,
Forms an inverted lily, earthward facing,
Petals wide-spread as though opening
In response to the long-departed figure
Kneeling on the cavern floor. Its span
Declares: here began the thaw from
Spellbound Moon to Easter Sun.

Birthplace

The Church of the Nativity

From one cave to another. Nazareth
To Bethlehem. Steps down and up.
And these not railed off. A long
Slow-moving queue among wealth
Of jeweled iconic glitter; the way
Emperors declared their faith,
Seventeen centuries lapsed. And still
People queue in the square outside,

Stoop beneath the stone lintel set
At a child's height; enter the interior
To queue at the other end, lowering
Heads again, two or three at a time
To squeeze on through, descend
Into the cave of birth. Here, the place
Marked by a star, here the manger,
The animals in that cavernous space.

My eyes suddenly fill with tears.
I don't know whether to cry or laugh.
It's joy's amazement. That such
A birth (and who knows whether here
Or in some other place?) could turn
The World so upside-down that
Every head might wear a crown!
Joy, like to a homecoming, the cave-

Like chambers of my heart echoing
With centuries of shared devotion
Here, while the World's uproar
Storms on by. *Here,* a few brief tears
Of joyful recognition, before being
Ushered on and out by so many
More of us pressing in from the long
 Slow-moving queues outside.

Bethlehem

Midwinter's peaceful interlude
Of collective wish-fulfilment
Close-held to hearts world-wide
In carol service, cathedral choir.

Blossoming of the Christmas rose:
Bethlehem! *how still we see thee lie.*
Such hopes projected onto these
Rocky slopes where urban sprawl

Now faces down the olive groves,
Old times fenced around alongside
Abandoned rubbish and scrap cars.
The future's promise beckons from

Adverts tall as a block of flats
And empty new apartments
For those favoured with the cash.
It's twilight. After hours. We're herded

Into a craft shop selling carvings
Of angels, animals, Bible stories
All in olive wood. The doors open
For us and close behind. Pilgrims'

Prerogative. Discounts all round.
We're sheep in a fold, browsing
In the mood of a peaceful interlude;
Pondering our Christmas gifts.

Creche Bethlehem

founded 1884

Creepy. The white wall of the apse
Bears down impassive-blank. I feel
I'm in a morgue. Christ hangs
On His cross polished to a fine finish,

While mounted in a niche on high
His Mother gazes down electric halo lit.
Incense reeks and a sticky-sweet web
Envelopes you. That smiling frown,

That sense of guilt ... Unease
Bordering on fear with its unsettling,
Suggestive power bears down to keep
You fenced about, fenced in. It's why

You have to free yourself, break out ...
We're ushered into a long corridor,
Disney characters on the walls,
The smell of disinfectant.

We're shown to a room dim-lit,
Blinds drawn. Twenty cots
Of abandoned children tucked up
Sleeping. One room of several.

From another, a carer brings a little one
Nine days old. The teenage mother's
Being protected from her family.
She's to blame, of course: outcast,

The shame collective, her child
Blighted from the start. Here is mercy,
Care, breathing space. But this child's
Adult future? And how long before

These tangling webs are blown away
On the Spirit's breath and Cross
And Crescent meet in the shared
Sovereignty of Love to birth
                    a better World?

Baptism

King Hussein's Bridge near Jericho

The land locked down and mined. Armed guards
Either side of the brown stream. A boundary
Where differences meet, flow into one another,

Or collide. And here: in open water bordered
By reeds, people in white gowns are taking turns
To fall back into reassuring arms, be lowered

Briefly, into the water, face up (some with
A flannel to cover nose and mouth); then
Be raised to singing and applause. We stand

Apart, English, Anglican, soberly looking on.
What if John were suddenly to appear, take us all
By storm, on fire with the Messianic Promise

At hand? And Jesus, next in the queue, were taking
His turn for no symbolic dip and we, so gripped
With John's compelling force, had no eyes for Him

Emerging, dripping, soaked as any other humble
God-fearing convert raised from their immersion,
No eyes for the Christ, the newly anointed One,

    Only for John. Fiery, wild-clad Prophet.
        The real thing, come alive!

Welcome Home

Nazareth: one Sabbath in
the Synagogue. Luke 4, 16-30

He's back. But no longer as the one
Who left. The glitter, now, of stardust
That clings to him! The stories
That keep flooding in; and here he is.
In the very place he learned to read.

All eyes on him as he's handed
The scroll for this Sabbath's reading.
The spirit of the Lord..has anointed me.
To bring the good news to the poor.
His bearing! The ring of his voice!

As he sits, the awed silence speaks
Of heart-felt pride as though they
Own a part of him, being local.
And wouldn't they love to see
For themselves those wonders

They've heard so much about!
This text is being fulfilled today, even
As you listen. He's on his feet again
Responding to the admiring swell
Of misplaced wishes and wonderings.

What follows touches a raw nerve
Such as scatters any glints of star-
Dust still impeding sight: unsettling
Home-truths puncturing complacent
Pride in being God's Chosen Ones.

There's uproar. He's hustled outside,
Hauled up flights of steps to the brow
Of the town's hilltop until, surging
To its sheer brink, everyone crowds
To a standstill and headstrong rage

Gives way to silence as though
Suddenly becalmed. Only then
And without a word, he asserts
His will. Folk step aside, some
Shamefaced? As he slips through

And walks away.

Jerusalem BC/AD

The Garden Sepulchre

    Floats over an abyss

Put your ear to a fissure in the rock,
You'll hear far below the sound
Of rushing waters, the earth torn wide,

Once restless with billowing steam
And fumes and sudden bursts of flame.
In later times, a ravine of Oracles.

In his wisdom, Solomon filled it in.

    And so it comes to pass

After a tumult of years, of cries
And hammerings, one subject
To the rule of Rome and put to death
Outside the city walls, is laid to rest

Within a garden-sepulchre nearby.

Throughout the night earth tremors
Shake the old divide, reopen glimpses
Into *Adam's grave*. As dawn breaks
And the tremors die away, a woman

In tears of bewildered grief stands asking
One she takes to be the gardener:
Where have you taken him?
               Tell me, where has he gone?

The Church of the Holy Sepulchre

Originally consecrated in September AD 335

>1

Hadrian's Podium

Rising ground visible
From the city walls.
Rock-hewn tombs

And a disused quarry
Convenient for public
Executions. A century

Goes by and Rome's
Rebuilding Jerusalem,
This the site chosen

To be covered with
An imposing podium,
Veneration directed

To where it rightfully
Belongs: Jupiter, Venus.
It doesn't last. What's

Been impressed here
On hill and empty tomb
Is a future that will

Supplant the imperial
Reach of Rome.

2

Constantine's Basilica

Two more centuries pass.

Hadrian's podium is cleared
To uncover what remains
Of that *most blessed spot:*

An isolated rock amidst
An open space and tombs
Set into rising ground.

For building to begin the hillside's
Cut away. A large rotunda
Rises over the revered place

And opens into a cloister
Embracing what remains
Of Golgotha. The summit's

Levelled off. A cross erected
And a metal grille; finally,
Extending east: Constantine's

Basilica; while in a cistern
Lower down the hill, his mother
Uncovers the True Cross

And relics of the Passion.
    The reign of
Christ Imperial begins.

3

Christendom's Most Holy Shrine

Heaven, hell and purgatory
Are reflected here: peace
And love in liturgy, in hand

A sword. Destroyed, rebuilt
Repeatedly, woven into
The fabric of the State,

The Tomb hacked to pieces,
Outraged Crusaders
Up to the hilt in blood.

Earthquakes still may shake
Both rock and sepulchre
And fire turn renovation

Into iconoclastic revenge.
All that hate conspires
To reject or understanding

Prompts to reconcile finds
Expression here. And ever
Since Crusaders lost Jerusalem,

The keys to lock, unlock
Their most holy shrine
Have been in the zealous

(Jealous?) keeping of the same
   Two Muslim families

4

November 2018

The wide entrance pours
Into sunlight the interior dark.
Inside: perpetual ebb and flow;
The place of the Anointing
Crowded with people waiting
To kneel, touch, move on,
Climb the stairs to what remains
Of Golgotha, (cased under glass)
Or join another queue around
The alabaster shrine enclosing
The site of the Holy Sepulchre.

Ritual marks the canonical Hours,
Monks forming facing lines
At one station, tapers lit to illumine
The texts of chants, moving on
To the next, crowds in tow:
Orthodox, Catholic, Armenian..
Each to their own and shared spaces
Under the one roof; with the cistern
Of the True Cross, the cave
Of Adam; mythic beginnings
Merging into World history,
BC to AD, the future pressing in
On this constant movement,
Crossing, recrossing between
The poles of willing sacrifice
And life's renewal; necessities
In hand (cameras, iPhones
Held aloft) and sacred space

Enlarging or diminishing
In human hearts world-wide?

Tabgha

The Sea of Galilee near Capernaum

The fish still like it here. The Sea's warmed
By thermal vents and fed by seven springs.
They multiply, satisfying human needs
With more to spare. Nearby's the setting
For the story of the multiplying Loaves.

Dawn's breaking. They're back to the old life
And a fruitless night out fishing. As they approach
The shore, a stranger hails them, telling them
To cast their nets on the other side, and the fish
Pour in beyond all imaginings. It's breakfast-time,

Served on this granite stone now walled about
By *Peter's Primacy,* a chapel of black volcanic rock.
Love, like Science, must also break the mould
When the time is ripe; be the way to truth
When truth cannot be spoken for reasons

Of commercial reputation, loss of power,
Of profits. And who else but Love to heal
The up-welling springs of sub-natural realms
Inimical to life? Or the radiant arrays, world-wide
Whose misuse casts long shadows that blight

The innocence of childhood and plunge into
Obsessive gloom the budding hopes of youth?
Science knows neither brakes nor reverse gears
When driven by competing interests; closes ranks
In deference to the powers funding its research.

When dawn finally begins to break, will it show
A World bereft, devastated, with nowhere else
To hide? Or ears, hearts, minds more open
To the Voice calling from the shore, bidding us
Turn about and cast our nets over the other side?

Times and Places

Walk in February

Westhide, Herefordshire

The air's so fine, the light so full
Of clarity, so high on promises
Of what's to be, we could
Mistake our own mortality,
Sauntering among the snowdrops
In this country churchyard, time
Held in the light's suspense.

We turn the weighty iron knocker,
Cross into the church's silence.
Flagstones worn by centuries of feet.
An alabaster slab from Tudor times,
Sixteen children ranked in line.
Carved effigy in a recess: a figure
From the Middle Ages, feet resting
On his dog, and on the wall,
The old bell wheel that might
Have tolled his death. And so—
Back to Domesday and beyond...

Or fast forwards, as we step
Into the morning light and there
The National School already
Closed by 1902, or the canal
Along the road once laid to rail,
Long since fallen into disuse
And now returned to a Canal Trust
For partial restoration and reuse.

To and fro; ebb and flow; year
Succeeding year, change
Upon change. And the light's
Clarity, once more brimful,
                              outpoured

Man on Wire

*Phillipe Petit's celebrated wire walk
between the Twin Towers
on 7th August, 1974*

It's a new day and eyes are drawn
From the dead-ahead up, up.
Can you see? It takes time to focus.
Then disbelief. A night-spun thread

Linking the fated Towers and a figure
There, there in the impossible between.
The giddy Twins are racing the clouds
While he kneels, stands, pirouettes

On his one-inch wire: a dance of life
At its utmost edge. He's called to come
Down but he won't, regulations
Tumbling with every studied step,

Scattering on the early morning air
In glorious confusion. It's a wire walk
To the brink of ourselves. Arresting
The Dead-Ahead with a cleaving shaft

    Of the Vertical.

Royal Wedding

*The Wedding of Prince William
and Kate Middleton April 29 2011*

It's an ambush. But how willingly
We're overpowered, taken prisoner,
Drawn captive to fairy-tale palaces
As if that's where our sovereign selves
Truly belong! And after all it's one

Of us they've kidnapped, one of us
About to step into that carriage
Drawn by four white horses. And-
It's all arisen by touches of magic:
Of eyes, of hearts, hands, lips.

All this panoply of fanfares, of kings
And queens and heads of state:
Are we dreaming or awake?
All assembled as witnesses
Of a promise to be exchanged.

Their love has caused real trees
Complete with Spring's regalia
To spring up overnight along
The abbey nave and now their every
Glance and smile is taken as refreshment –

Silver rain, golden showers- and her
Dream wedding dress, its silken train
Trailing the red carpet all the way
To the far end where a forest bank
Of blossoms and greenery awaits.

It leaves the commentators short
Of breath. And all they have to do
Is smile, show their joy and watching
Millions go wild with cheering,
Moist-eyed, as if it's one of their own

They're seeing on the big screen,
One of their own they've cradled
Who now stands tall carrying their
Hopes and dreams. What an ambush!
The nation's conquered heart, a proud

Parent flooded to overflowing
                      with royal wealth.

Let's Riot

London, August 2011

The glee on those youthful faces.
What a lark! Glass splinters into
Spider-patterns, then caves in
Under black boots. Fire follows.

Its flare and crackle is demonic joy:
Burn, burn; they're on fire too,
In gang-heaven, wrong and right
Going up in smoke, sparks

Disappearing into the night sky.
Reason's blindfolded, easy
To dodge. There's safety in numbers,
Adrenalin rush. Every stoved-in

Window is a gate-crashed threshold
Into dream-chaos come true. Over-
Run of primitive Will, grabbing stuff
And making off. What a lark!

We look on in disbelief. Our children
Broken loose, ducking under
The bar of the Law, in their wake,
Burning debris, broken businesses,

People homeless. Have our reserves
Of moral capital sunk this low?
Left too long unused to depreciate
Or rather, transferred to fund

Unending growth of the very goods,
The stuff, the *having to have,* these kids
Have burnt and rampaged for?

The Hallelujah Chorus

Hereford Cathedral, Christmas 2008

Without prompting, everybody stands!
Respect of centuries' long-standing
Through empires, wars, revolutions-

To the risen phoenix of material
Prosperity and multiplying shadows
Masking the sense of who we are.

But here's one jolting moment of recall
Of what it means to be British:
To stand up for the Hallelujah Chorus!

(Or- refusing that, to opt for a ride
In Blake's Chariot of Fire seeing
Jerusalem has not arrived despite

The profits and annual performances
Of the *Messiah.)*

      AND LORD OF ALL...

Soprano voices rising to vaults once built
To span a kingdom's vision before the rise
Of the Nation State;

    LORD OF LORDS...

Thunder the basses notwithstanding the vision's
Sea-change to needful habits of consumption,
Waste and greed.

    AND HE SHALL REIGN
    FOR EVER AND EVER...

    The Hallelujah Shock!

Everybody stirred to their feet by habitual
Deferrence to a long-dead king?

                      Or *Hallelujah's*
Power to launch us free of the magnetic
Pull of back-lit glitter and the acquisitive

Power of Things?

Golden Wedding

for Andrew, Linda, Stephanie
and in memory of Martyn who died
following a fall from a road bridge
in September 2002

Brother, captured striding to be married
In a winning year. I'm in my teens,
Bobby Moore's shoulder-high with the trophy.

And now it's the Olympics fifty years on
And we're all retired and crowding a restaurant
To celebrate. Your starting circle's still

Intact and rippled wide: a surprise arrival
From Europe, acclamations from Africa.
Top of the podium! Double gold or is it

Triple? For there's Stephanie too, the three
Of you a blink of fourteen years ago
Entered for one of life's greatest trials:

To ignite a living flame
                      from the heart of loss.

Fawley Church

How Caple, Herefordshire

At the end of a muddy track,
A sign to the left to keep
Would-be visitors out of the farmyard.

A dog raises the hue and cry
As you spot the building and bricked-in
Doorway with its Norman arch.

What's to be seen once
You've discouraged the dog
And found the real door

Is a floor as old as the Crusades,
A tub font predating the Conquest,
A raftered barn of a place

Now largely redundant
But for a few yearly services.
One more empty House of God,

Bourne along through the generations
By that solidarity of belief,
Duty, practice now crumbling

As surely as would these walls
Were due care to be withdrawn.

*

Three Norman arches frame
The chancel, portals which create
A feeling of inner as well as

Outer space. Stained glass windows
Cast the light into coloured stories,
Shift the focus from the farmyard world

Outside, to altar, candle, cross.
The place transmutes into your own
Inner space, into eloquent stillness:

And what breaks through
Like the sudden onrush of spring
Along a wintering bough

Is blossom, showered blessings,
Immaterial confetti – no, not
For some especial couple's wedding

But for an endless celebration
Of all who will. For what is
An altar if not tomb and table,

And what is the heart if not the space
Where thanks are offered and bread
Is broken with the Lord of Love,

With the living – and the dead.

'Les Etangs' Revisited

In the Swiss Alps near Champery

World's end, where the road runs out
At the forest's fringe near the trout pools;
Constant roar of the mountain torrent.

Silence otherwise. Cut logs stacked

Precisely, sheltered under corrugated iron
As years before, but not the same logs;
Who wants woodworm to take hold?

All changes here and remains the same.
Decades must count as fleeting seconds
For this sheer austere face of rock

Towering above the tall pines needle-
Dense and dark, withdrawn into a past
Where volleys of fractured rock

In giant blocks have been loosed, torn
Free to crash headlong onto the valley floor.
Earth tremors? Glacial weathering?

Colossal wreckage now at rest,
Each its own tumbled world softened
By mosses, lichen, fern, saplings

Taking root in cracks and crevices

*

It's late September. An afternoon
Of cloudless blue. Shadows
Lengthen across the mowed
Meadow-lawn of the family's
Holiday chalet; once, the structure
Stabling their cows and hay.

And how we come to be here- (I
By marriage into the family)-
Moving chairs to linger longer
In the sun, conscious of a cold
Touch as its declining rays
Dip behind the pines, warmth

Withdrawn and that sudden
Chill, breathing refreshment
Of the torrent's roar- how we
Come to be here basking in
This wealth of place- is because
An immemorial way of life,

Enclosed, like these pines,
Within their rooted self-
Sufficient selves, has fallen
Out of favour with the young,
Where land's no longer
The tie binding you to home,

But that scarce and prized
Commodity not for growing
Your own food, but to be
Traded in to ensure a secure
Financial bedrock for your life.

*

Look up. The bare-faced rock's
Lit up in relief. There's a thread
Of ledge you can walk along,

While higher, root-clasped
On overhangs, small pines lean
Precariously. And- suddenly,

For the space of a heart-beat,
A soundless, breeze-filled sail,
Orange against the blue,

Dips behind the tree-line
Its rider's sight fixed, no doubt,
On the fluttering wind-sock

Marking the place in the meadows
Far below where cones are set out
For the target landing space.

*

Pause here?
               Or continue

Looking up? For reaching
Beyond all this, is a far off
Summit, a peak outlined

In the haze, of which this
Grey rock face would be
The merest detail.

And what appears
To shape-shifting sight,
Is the vast profile

Of another Face, reclining,
Awake or dreaming,
In endless contemplation

Of unseen skies.

Notes and Acknowledgements

Crop Circle: grateful acknowledgements to the account in Lucy Pringle's *Crop Circles The Pitkin Guide 2004 pp 10/11*

Crop Circle: Aerial View: grateful acknowledgements to Francine Blake for the aerial photograph from the *Crop Circle Calendar 2008 (November)*

Augustine's Chair
See Bede's *A History of the English Church and People Book 2 Chapter 2.*
Augustine urged the Celtic (British) Church to join with the Roman Church in (among other matters of difference) missionary work among the unconverted English. As the British could not bring themselves to accept Augustine's authority, he issued his warning, the prophetic element of which was, that if they failed to convert the unconverted, they would likely fall their victims. This eventually came true when an English army turned on the monks of Bangor and slaughtered them for praying for the British side of the battle.
For details concerning the Chair used in this meeting see *Finding Augustine's Chair James Johnston 1898* (the Chair was rescued from a bonfire!).

Undelivered: see Appian: *The Civil Wars, Book 2, 57*